1,001

Ways to Decorate with What You Love

1,001
Ways to Decorate with What You Love

Vanessa-Ann

Sterling Publishing Co., Inc. New York
A Sterling/Chapelle Book

Chapelle, Ltd.:
Jo Packham
Sara Toliver
Cindy Stoeckl

Editor: Ray Cornia
Editorial Director: Caroll Shreeve
Art Director: Karla Haberstich
Graphic Illustrator: Kim Taylor
Copy Editor: Marilyn Goff
Staff: Burgundy Alleman, Areta Bingham, Susan Jorgensen,
  Emily Kirk, Barbara Milburn, Lecia Monsen, Karmen Quinney,
  Desirée Wybrow

If you have any questions or comments, please contact:
Chapelle, Ltd., Inc., P.O. Box 9252, Ogden, UT 84409
    (801) 621-2777 • (801) 621-2788 Fax
    e-mail: chapelle@chapelleltd.com
    web site: www.chapelleltd.com

Library of Congress Cataloging-in-Publication Data:

1, 001 ways to decorate with what you love.
      p. cm.
   "A Sterling/Chapelle Book."
   Includes index.
   ISBN 0-8069-9925-X
   1. Interior decoration. I. Title: One thousand one ways to decorate with what you love. II. Title: One thousand and one ways to decorate with what you love.
NK2110.A17 2003
747--dc21

                                        2002155315

10 9 8 7 6 5 4 3 2 1

Published by Sterling Publishing Co., Inc.
387 Park Avenue South, New York, NY 10016
©2003 by Jo Packham
Distributed in Canada by Sterling Publishing
c/o Canadian Manda Group, One Atlantic Avenue, Suite 105
Toronto, Ontario, Canada M6K 3E7
Distributed in Great Britain by Chrysalis Books
64 Brewery Road, London N7 9NT, England
Distributed in Australia by Capricorn Link (Australia) Pty. Ltd.
P.O. Box 704, Windsor, NSW 2756, Australia
Printed and Bound in China
All Rights Reserved

Sterling ISBN 0-8069-9925-X

Introduction

The joy of decorating any home or garden comes in making an envisioned image a reality. It helps tremendously to be clear about what sort of styling "feel" and visual appearance one is seeking to achieve. Sometimes, only the spark of an idea is all it takes to begin something as simple as a rearrangement of furniture and decorative items that may already exist on the premises or as exciting as an entirely new decorating scheme.

This book of *1,001 Ways to Decorate with What You Love* is guaranteed to provide home and garden decorators with fresh suggestions for styling old treasures, creating special faux treatments, and selecting new purchases with imagination and unique personal vitality.

Moving a chair to a different location, stacking a smaller table on top of a larger table, setting up a focal-point arrangement of treasured belongings on a bookshelf, in a corner, on a stair landing, or up on the mantelpiece can result in a satisfying "lift" to the ambience of any room in your home or outdoor garden space.

The book is organized into styling sections with specific theme ideas for garden and interior home styling.

Whether your tastes run toward the sleek and severe in minimal styling, the traditional approaches from country to classic high-style, or the eclectic mixes of a variety of inspirations, *1,001 Ways to Decorate with What You Love* has some new styling help for your enthusiasms.

Here you will find tips on making a particular theme work as you organize, arrange, and style the garden and every room in your home. Suggestions for faux treatments of walls, floors, furnishings, and garden accessories are given in specific directives.

Groupings of items for emphasis and comfort are included for small focal points on shelves and mantels and for organizing entire spaces to set a consistent style approach. With more than a thousand pictures and caption directions to select from, there's a delightful idea here just waiting to enhance your space.

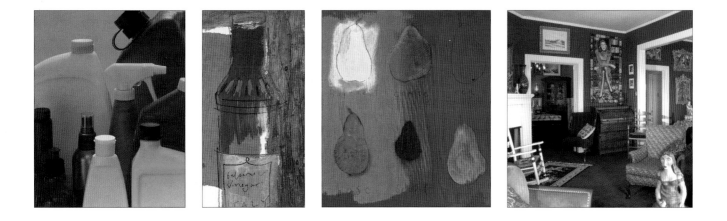

Table of
Contents

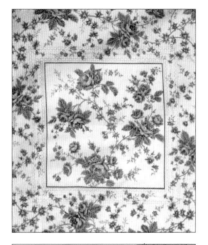

Asian
Style

An Asian theme is all about the seamless relationship between nature, tools, and creativity. To the Eastern mind, creativity is a sacred process. Appreciating beauty cannot be separated from daily living and one's most basic utensils and decorative accessories. To appreciate and cultivate beauty is to breathe and live and work, continuing the sacred circle. Decorating in the Asian style is a thoughtful and a spiritual process. Respect for materials and craftsmanship is paramount. Heaven, man, and earth symbols can be expressed with a tall flower, a mid-height flower, and a very low one, perhaps floating in water. Telling a story with items combined in a focal-point arrangement is a delightful exercise.

Natural materials are basic to Oriental aesthetics. Bamboo, silk, metal, wood, clay, stone, even water have both symbolic and decorative power to express beauty and meaning in the home and garden. Colors and textures are always in harmony with natural materials. Strong forms, colors, and textures as well as subtle ones are important.

Asian Style

Use Oriental calligraphy, symbolic of meanings you hold dear, for theme fabrics and wall coverings.

Collected pieces that you may have used outdoors can be the perfect dramatic touch for an entryway.

Place large vases on an oversized stair step to bring attention to an area that needs a transition.

Asian craftsmanship is notably elegant in its smallest detail. Group similar items and tie with red cord.

Sumptuous patterned fabrics with border designs harmonize well if used in color families.

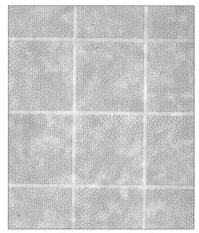

Ceramic tiles in nature's palette are a suitable background for floors or walls in Oriental-themed areas.

Make red the prevalent color in Pacific Rim-style rooms with bowls of seeds, beads, fruits, and flowers.

Use stylized floral prints on black backgrounds for textiles and wall coverings.

Group cast-metal collectibles for table-setting focal points. Float a fresh blossom in a bowl of sauce.

Mount a wastebasket or box with one flat side to the wall, accent with tassels, and use as a vase.

Fancy Asian-style hardware can make an aged wooden box a collectible trunk to use for storage.

Create a hall table by attaching two stone corbels to a wall and adding a glass shelf for small items.

Use bookshelves as a place to display favorite pieces of art by leaning them against the books.

Tree branches can be displayed by themselves or they can be used to feature seasonal accents.

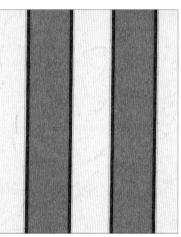

Wide-striped wallpaper can be used to paper the back of a bookcase to add color and interest.

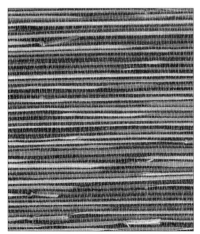

Grass and bamboo cloth with a colored background can be used to cover walls or enhance furniture.

Small printed scenes from Asian-theme vintage wallpaper can be framed in antique frames.

Display collections of small treasures by lining them evenly on shelves or a lacquered tabletop.

Asian *Style*

Use a high stone wall in the garden as a trellis to train espalier trees and beautiful climbing vines.

Build a small stone patio to support a wooden bench in a hidden conversation corner of the garden.

Steep hills become intriguing when stone stairs are built to lead upward to a mysterious destination.

Grass walkways in the center of stone patios are a contradiction that adds texture and color.

Hidden statues are usually indicative of places that are peaceful and can be used as sanctuaries.

Create a radiating stone circle in the center of a patio and place a favored tree or statue at its center.

Walkways can be made by placing small stones or bricks evenly among patches of ground cover.

Vintage stone statuary at the top of a garden stairway creates ancient appeal inviting further exploration.

Grow unexpected flowers in the center of a garden that has a theme in which they cause surprise.

Prop a framed Oriental print against a wall or bookcase shelf; secure it off-center with a tiny pot.

Make wall art by sponge-painting light brick shapes on a dark textured background—then glaze.

Place a small arrangement of nature materials and boxes before a mirror to double theme impact.

Shadow-box frames are ideal to hold an Asian-themed arrangement of nature-related objects.

Pair two shadow-boxes of framed art made from handmade paper and 3-D items for a bold statement.

Tell a story—as this monkey atop a trunk does, who appears to have reached for beads nearby.

Small unique furniture pieces and in-scale displays pack style punch for stair landings and foyers.

Gold-filigree motifs of leafy branches against black are elegant for wall coverings and draperies.

Create drama with black and gold stripes for pillows, upholstery, or wallpaper accents in dining areas.

Bamboo-themed wallpaper designs with vining plants can give a trel-lised-garden effect to a sun room.

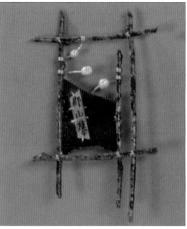

Minimal design uses related colors and treats "empty" shelves as shapes of equal weight to objects.

Tie twigs frame-style with cord. Embellish with stamped paper, feathers, images, and beads.

Hang a calligraphy-print drop shade in earth tones and tie it with a cord and large wooden beads.

To add an Asian influence, lean a framed piece against the wall and place a round gold bowl in front.

Use a discarded log with its bark chiseled off and one end polished as a side "table," indoors or out.

Use twigs, found objects, or small treasures to create Oriental wall hangings large or small.

Display framed art with tiny col-lectibles on a bookshelf for a charming miniature art gallery.

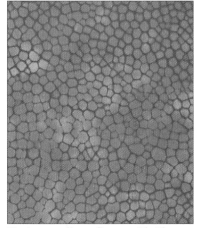

Texture walls or floors with tile or create a faux finish using tape and stamps or sponge-painted effects.

Ginger jars in harmonizing colors combine well with Oriental trays and a carved-wood stand.

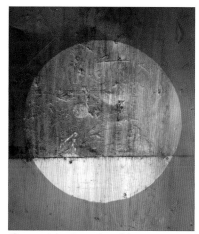

Geometrics in painted layers are elegantly simple for an entry wall or the exit to a "moon" garden.

An ornamental tree, shogi screen, and red-painted "beam" treatment welcome to a serene garden room.

Simplicity, always present in Asian decorating, is represented by these two unlabeled bottles of oil.

Place soap, robe, and slippers on a simple stool beside your bath for beauty-ritual accessibility.

Windows into the garden for walls above the kitchen counter mean styling should be kept simple.

Arrange books by color, height, or subject and decorate bookshelves with favorite keepsakes.

Old water containers are easily restored with a coat of paint and decoupaged magazine pictures.

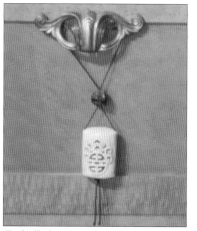

Embellish a simple box or chest with vintage hardware and hang a beaded cord for elegant details.

Asian *Style*

Make art out of ice cream in a tilted bowl with sugar "chopsticks" and a paper umbrella.

A small wooden chest can be used as a backdrop to display Oriental fans and origami art.

A candle on a metal stand sets river-run stones aglow, with stamped calligraphy for balance.

Hang an ivory Oriental keepsake from the finial of a lamp so that it adds exotic interest to the shade.

Ornamental fabrics can be used to make pillows, to drape over a chair back, or to lay across a table.

A carved Oriental lantern brings an empty corner the light of design style. Embellish with foliage.

Statuettes can be collected and displayed on tabletops or by themselves on top of a small stool.

To serve meals with an Oriental flavor, cover the table with scripted wrapping paper or a newspaper.

Oriental cards framed and embellished can be used in decorating for any season of the year.

Cast-off Oriental-style trays are often found at flea markets and can be used for display or serving.

For meals that require chopsticks, use traditional square plates on a wooden tabletop.

Oriental-style lanterns that are originally purchased for outdoors can make a bold statement inside.

When using chopsticks add an Oriental touch to the service by attaching jewelry as napkin rings.

Add a Chinese tasseled button to an Oriental pouch of metallic-stamped fabric of silk or rayon.

For Oriental dinners, place persimmon branches on the table for a simple yet beautiful detail.

Lily ponds are easy to make inside or out. For a special party, fill your hot tub with floating water lilies.

Design your spring plantings simply in color and type to depict the serenity of Oriental gardens.

Protective walls can be softened by planting easy-to-grow foliage adjacent to where people might walk.

French Country_
Style

A kitchen in the French style would hardly be authentic without a French pot rack within easy reach. A French-provincial desk and a bentwood café chair add romance to a red wall and charming tabletop accents. Chinese-red accents were popular in the Impressionist period, so design with them freely. A wine cellar in the French tradition calls for a tasting session on the premises, so decorate the room as another intimate entertainment area in your home. Be sure to use dimmers and candles for French ambience.

French bottles and other "*en français*" labeled items add a nostalgic touch to a focal point. A white rococo fireplace is extra dramatic when the beams are painted to match in contrast to ruby-toned walls and ceilings. Coffee-table books of French artists and musicians can become focal points in themselves. Pick up the theme on the cover with fruits, fruit-shaped candles, flowers, and jars to extend the picture's subject matter into the foreground. Such a grouping of related objects and colors makes for great conversation.

Stack creamy white cups in a curvy wire basket for easy access and a sense of casual playfulness.

On a bedroom dresser, fold a vintage bedspread accompanied by a candle with harmonizing colors.

Fashion a simple wreath of boxwood to accent a sweet pair of bird figurines on shelf, mantel, or sill.

Note like an artist the subtle shades in nature's palette, when choosing colors for a decorating scheme.

Scatter life-like art among everyday items to bring beauty of form and texture to common-place activities.

Old French flower cans may be hung on a wall in a single or a double row or placed on shelftops.

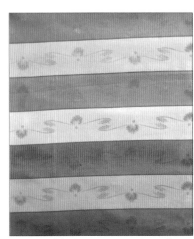

Vintage fabrics can sometimes be purchased in like but different patterns so they can be used together.

A plain green wall can be changed to several different shades by applying a light-colored glaze.

Emphasize vibrancy in a garden by planting flowers of strongly contrasting colors and textures.

During an ordinary weeknight, decorate the dining-room table as if company were coming.

Large images from wallpaper can be cut and decoupaged onto furniture pieces to accent a room.

Fresh tulips in a metal vase accent a distressed-wood mirror frame and a mounted vintage card.

Arrange a charming decorative birdhouse with a candle, some beach items, and fresh wildflowers.

Line candles in an even row, having only one candle a different color from the others for surprise.

Striped wallpaper and floral wallpaper that contain the same colors can be pleasingly combined.

Faux-finish plastic fruit with acrylic paints so that their appearance is natural and luscious.

Bright- or bold-colored wallpapers can be muted by washing with a diluted paint of the same color.

Traditionally, odd numbers are used in decorating, but try an even number for a change.

A ribbon rose can be pinned to the center of a satin pillow to add an elegant romantic touch.

Arrange jars of syrup on kitchen shelves the same way they would be in an exclusive French shop.

Place a small bouquet of paper flowers next to the pillow on a beautifully made bed.

Match several garden accents on indoor shelving units. Distress both the shelves and the pots.

A garden-themed wallpaper can be used either inside the house or outside on the wall of a patio.

Arrange food and flowers with unexpected items to add sculptural interest to small arrangements.

Use small-print wallpaper that is made to complement larger prints on insides of hutches or cabinets.

Paint all of the furniture in one room the same color and add accents with one additional color.

Cover wooden frames with wrapping paper and embellish with pieces of ribbon and old buttons.

A wrought-iron chair and table can be placed in the garden so that they are only for theme display.

Replace an ordinary gate with a vintage gate and border with large bushes on both sides.

While traveling, sketch areas and scenes that you love, then frame and hang them at home.

Hint at a more leisurely pace of life by propping a vintage bicycle against the garage or garden wall.

Employ a sense of humor and adventure when adding a personal touch to decorative items.

Use unexpected accents like the hand above, to give humor and character to utilitarian spaces.

Mass simple wildflowers in an unusual planter to give casual appeal in the private garden.

Warm the home with the bright colors of the South of France for a cheerful, upbeat presence.

If you have a long pathway in your garden, plant masses of foliage down both sides for romance.

Hang a curvy wrought-iron gate in vintage style within a garden wall to hint at the beauty inside.

Allow moss to grow on old stone to give a feeling of timeless permanence and immovability.

An archway in the garden hides most of the view so there is a suggestion of mystery and adventure.

Allow for the sound of water in the garden to mask traffic noise and create a peaceful atmosphere.

Position an attractive bench for a pleasing view, providing opportunity for intimate conversation.

Train a vine to grow onto the facade of the home to mellow the exterior with graceful age.

Use a weathered balustrade to visually and physically separate the garden from the terrace.

Accent a rough brick fireplace with an old lamp-base "urn" that has been faux finished for texture.

Invite the garden onto the patio by using large pots of luxuriant plants to bridge spaces with foliage.

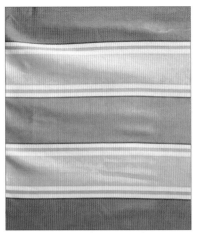

Striped vintage fabric can be a nice accent to all of the floral patterns that are used in French decorating.

A corner of your kitchen counter-top can be used as a "display" area for flowers and favorite bottles.

Small vintage crates can have wooden or papier-mâché cutouts attached as interesting accents.

Make the top of a chest of drawers a dramatic bar area by pairing two identical lamps on either side.

Select country fabrics that you like and make them appear French by selecting a French colourway.

Consider leaving your dishes on the table for charm and so that unexpected guests can be served.

Shades of green, brown, and orange bring earth tones for tiles, carpets, and upholstery.

Arrange a candle with molded foliage and a tile with a child's handprint for a place setting.

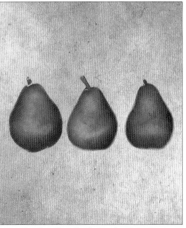

On the backsplash in the kitchen, stencil pears in an even row and highlight with a gold-tipped brush.

Wallpaper can be created by faux-finishing squares of brown wrapping paper and glazing a finish.

Spray two mismatched furniture pieces with white paint and accent with brightly colored hydrangeas.

French country-style window boxes burst with color and texture to soften the house's hard exterior.

Let flowers peek over the top of a rough outer wall for a hint of the garden's personality inside.

Let moss grow on a wooden bench in the garden and use it, not to sit on, but as focal-point garden art.

Paint a back door green in the summertime, then dark grey blue for the cool winter months.

Angelic statuettes are a spirited accent when placed in the garden, on the porch, or in the house.

Tuck a large earthenware pot with a lid for a "plant pedestal" in a garden corner for foliage height.

Create a tranquil garden setting with related muted colors in the plants, stonework, and statuary.

Drape yards of fabric around a decorative, seasonal, or faux fireplace. Remove them to light fire.

Match pairs of items such as lamps, sconces, and decorative items to tie together an eclectic decor.

Instill a sense of grandeur to a simple bathroom mirror by enhancing it with an elaborate gilt frame.

An inherited antique chair is a stunning style statement brought to attention by a bright throw.

Embellish a candle with sparkling beads. Arrange it with the glitter of glass and a small shiny frame.

Set a candle to reflect in an Art Nouveau "hand-me-down" mirror. A small bouquet adds interest.

Create variety in the height of arrangements by stacking pots on pedestals or upside-down bowls.

Show essential structural elements: wooden floors, brick walls, beams without adornment or drapery.

A twist on French country is all about minimal elements in maximum space, even for infants.

Pamper guests with indulgent toiletries in attractive bottles paired with luxurious towels.

For a change, do not fold your bathroom towels and hang them on the towel rack—drape them.

If you are having new tilework done and it is hand-painted, have the accessories painted to match.

A glass-topped white wooden farm table and more-formal chairs is a style contradiction that works.

An antique birdcage, with swagged windows, on a stand becomes a style setter, even without a bird.

Stage a countertop focal point with a grouping of dishes, sculpture, nature materials, and candles.

Encase a new or old tub in a tiled "seat" and backsplash for beauty and easy clean up.

Luxurious towels of different colors can be draped together making it easier to remember his and hers.

Double the effect of designer wallpaper with counter-to-ceiling mirror treatments and shower doors.

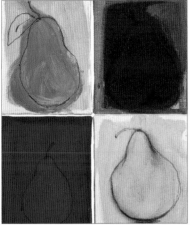

Country pears become styled images for wallpaper, tile, and stencil treatments you can create.

Cover kitchen shelf edges with "lace" cut from unusual papers, using decorative-edged scissors

Make traditional meals on the patio more of a celebration with edible blossoms, leaves, and herbs.

Create stained-glass mosaics for countertops, floor tiles, garden stepping stones, or food trivets.

Enjoy the charm of a French café with a bistro-style table and chairs in the dining room or on a patio.

Hang a sachet on a vintage door-knob so that the master or guest bedroom is scented at all times.

Lilacs and hydrangeas make a beautiful combination for a spring floral arrangement on a chair seat.

Hang a welcoming dried lavender wreath on the headboard of a guest-room bed to scent the room.

A hand-painted cake pedestal and glass dome can be used to display treasured or fragile items.

Store kitchen utensils that are used daily in marble jars that can be left sitting out on the countertop.

Lean a favorite antique print against the headboard on the bed in place of another pillow.

Fabrics and area rugs with strong nature elements form a rich background for period furniture.

Small jars of honey or syrup can be decorated for gift giving by adhering porcelain fruit to the lid.

Make a wreath from dried wheat that has been dyed unexpected colors and accent with silk flowers.

Vintage fabric can be used in kitchens that are either retro or more modern in design.

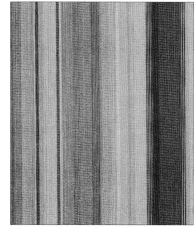

The simplicity of stripes is always welcome as a means of tying a room together by color and value.

Make your bed's duvet cover, pillow shams, and dust ruffle from the same prepleated silk fabric.

Printed fabrics can be enhanced for pillows or framing by sewing on beads to accent flowers.

Use an old sewing-machine cabinet as a focal point to display flowers on a covered patio or back porch.

Place a small makeup mirror on a cabinet top in stylish stacked style. Place it in front of framed art.

Use a flat basket filled with shells or other treasures to adorn a pretty bed during the daylight hours.

Give pillows a basket to rest in on a shelf in the bedroom or study so they are at hand for guest comfort.

Use muted blues and purples, French country colors reminiscent of Monet's Giverny paintings.

Hang a small girl's Easter bonnet on a frame that contains a photo of the hat being worn by a loved one.

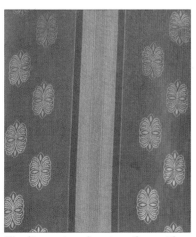

Tie disparate colors together with a common pattern to unify the overall look and feel of the room.

Warm yellow walls, framed tiles, and a primitive pottery statue tie a country kitchen together uniquely.

Build long open shelving in a kitchen. Display matched vintage containers and an old enamel scale.

For a temporary change, line the back of your kitchen cupboards with wall- or wrapping paper.

Vintage fabrics should be used for draperies and when upholstering furniture for restored rooms.

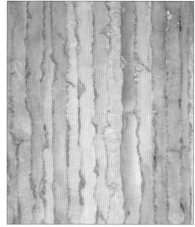

"Paper" a small area of a room by tearing strips of hand-dyed paper and adhering so they overlap.

Small "art" objects can be placed in the windowsill of the kitchen to enhance an ordinary view.

When not in use, drape a lamp's shade with a napkin, a lace doily, or a scarf.

When displaying handmade pillows, make certain to place them where they will not be leaned on.

Hang a grouping of plates and a round mirror above the bed to act as a charming "virtual" headboard.

For a slipcover that can be easily changed, drape a sheet over the chair and tuck under the cushions.

In the country garden, lavender and poppies are wonderfully old-fashioned for perennial beauty.

Place three chairs in a conversation area and two tall pedestals with dramatic plants between them.

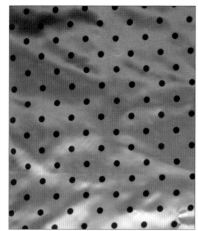

Use vintage polka-dot satin fabric as draperies, for pillows, and even for chair upholstery fabric.

A high-ceilinged room begs for architectural drama. Add massive furniture and bold color.

Place large overstuffed pillows against the backs of dining-room chairs for comfort and design.

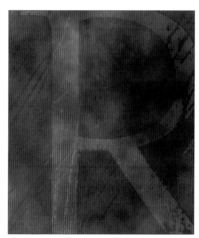

On one wall, stencil large letters and then wash the wall with several darker colors of paint or glaze.

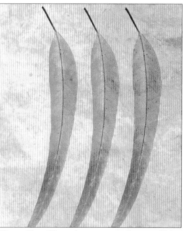

Stencil willow leaves on the wall in a hallway. They can be a normal size or exaggerated for effect.

Spice up mealtime with unique table settings to make everyday food and meals seem more exotic.

Make patched squares on bed quilts and pillow centers from matching oversized floral napkins.

A small alcove can be highlighted by adding an overhead light and "framing" with a garland.

Sometimes less is more as is the example here with a dining-room table that is always uncluttered.

On a library shelf use a small silver tray to hold candles arranged on each side of an antique ink well.

It is not always necessary to line the stairway with photographs, maybe a small grouping is better.

In a large room or between two, place chairs back to back to create individual conversation areas.

Obtain swatches of fabrics, wallpapers, and trims you like and then "live" with them for a while.

In a family room where space allows, place table and chairs for games behind the seating area.

Recall a bistro or café setting with a breakfast bar's cheery mugs and high-contrast chair cushions.

Stack favorite picture books and other treasures on a coffee table in a living room or study.

Hinged beveled mirrors can act as a small but dramatically reflecting backdrop on a dining-room buffet.

Lightly stencil floral and leaf patterns on light blue walls, then wash wall with several darker shades.

Etch windows behind a bar area to resemble glass doors that are the entryway to European cafés.

Choose your favorite colors from a variety of colored pencils and use those colors in your decorating.

Faux-finish a wall with a light wash, then stencil using real fern leaves and white paint.

Weathered white shutters and a bright red awning are a perfect backdrop for a window box.

When stenciling a wall, using real leaves as the stencil, add stem details with a permanent marker.

French posters can be mounted as a collage on a piece of posterboard and framed as a single art print.

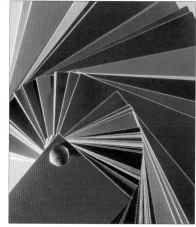

Always use a color wheel when selecting colors so they can be "placed" next to each other.

Fresh flowers make a perfect accent, whether in the garden or cut and brought inside.

English Country_
Style

The charm of chintz, pewter, and roses recalls misty London mornings, or evenings by the fire on the moors. Preparations for teatime themes and enjoying genteel comforts are basic to the style of any English country room or garden. Whether horseback riding is actually a pastime or you find riding gear in a flea market, what's more British than "riding to the hounds" and enjoying a "spot" of tea afterward?

Styled with attention to detail, floral porcelains and fabrics, tiles and carpets, echo a London town home, castle, or "flat." Recall the sea-merchant days of the British Empire with model schooners or fully rigged sailing ships in small vignettes on the mantelpiece.

Small antique clocks, enameled tiles, and a bevy of pretty containers bring the sparkle of the British Isles to traditional room design. Add good books in leatherbound editions and handmade lace. "Top off" with fine silver and jaunty pots of roses.

An English cottage opens into a garden. Bring the flowers indoors with wallpaper and fabric designs.

Lean an empty vintage picture frame on a shelf and line three of the same shape of candle in front.

Use green and yellow garden-colored stripes on one wall to complement floral wallpapers.

Baskets of rolled face cloths or hand towels make easy access a stylish invitation in the bath.

Tassels are stunning on drawers, lamps, pillows. Accent wallpaper and fabric with tassel borders.

Personalize a simple metal frame with a piece of jewelry or a vintage ornament glued in place for accent.

Underscore a casual arrangement of garden flowers by placing it in a weathered container on a ledge.

A picnic can be elegant in the back-yard, using your nice wine glasses and pretty linens to celebrate.

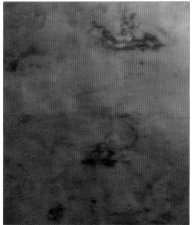

Ideas for unusual wall finishes are easy to obtain by copying the designs found on wrapping paper.

Damask dish towels can be used for tablecloths, chair-back covers, or framed as textured art.

Group vintage pictures on a wall with antique coat hooks and a salvaged towel bar for embroidery.

Use objects for different purposes: a pitcher for a flower vase, lace tablecloth or bedspread for drapes.

Buy old books at a flea market for classical display with statuary and other "literary" collectible pieces.

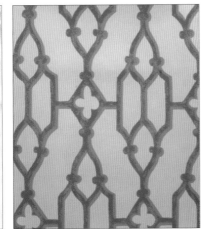

Lattice- or fretwork-style wallpaper takes on an English cottage theme in a traditional setting.

An old music stand is a nice way to display an open book on a shelf in the library or on top of a piano.

Use your favorite art or travel book as a pedestal to showcase your favorite lamp with style.

Books do not always have to be neatly stacked on bookshelves—arrange randomly with art objects.

Hang one picture on a wall, then stack one directly in front of it and one to the side on a shelf.

"Build shelves" by stacking benches on top of one another in front of a window. Accent with pottery.

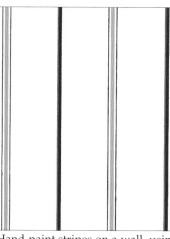

Hand-paint stripes on a wall, using different colored markers and a ruler. Wash over with glaze.

Paint a design on the top of an old wooden table or cover the table with wallpaper, then shellac it.

Use natural-patterned wallpaper and garden furniture to decorate a small cottage room with big style.

An old clock that may have been handed down from a grandparent is a perfect English Country accent.

Wallpaper can be made to appear vintage by washing with a thinned layer of taupe or gold paint.

Have abstract posters enlarged as textured graphics and paste them in place of traditional wallpaper.

Stagger frames on a shelf in layers, using a variety of styles and shapes but a common color or theme.

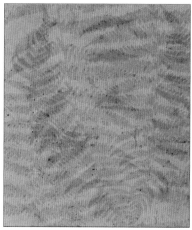

Using a diluted acrylic paint and a fern leaf as the stamp, "print" a soft green wallpaper, then glaze.

Plant flowers with a mounding habit in groups to accent a lush garden that is in bloom all year.

Set the stage for quiet moments of reflection with a wooden bench placed in a lush, secluded spot.

White hydrangea surrounded by blue delphiniums are perfect corner accents in any country garden.

Blend a palette of only one or two colors to cast attention on a stone statuette in the garden's center.

Nasturtiums give variety in leaf shapes and textures and their trumpet-like blossoms are edible.

Ornamental berry bushes are easy to grow in a country garden that is allowed to become overgrown.

Plant espalier trees to act as a backdrop in visual layers for the shorter plants against the garden fence.

Plant herbs for wonderful aroma in the garden, and in kitchen containers for cooking flavor indoors.

Soften the hard edges of an entry by hanging a welcoming basket of flowers from an ornate hook.

Layer a large empty frame over a smaller framed piece and place a very small framed piece in front.

Paint built-ins and furniture in a kitchen an off-white, then distress to keep a shabby-chic influence.

Arrange all-white serving pieces behind white cabinet doors to create a feeling of quiet organization.

Red-print toile fabric is used for English Country decorating—be it stately palace or humble cottage.

Salvage a broken teapot for decorative use by replacing a broken spout with a piece of found coral.

A painted shelf can be added to an old radiator cover to create a display case for childhood treasures.

A cottage Christmas would not be complete without an oversized Santa in the center of the table.

Cover an antique chair in a bright, more contemporary, shiny silk and place it in front of the fireplace.

An all-white living room should have a Christmas tree that looks as if it were dusted with snow.

Stretch out a table runner and style it with a row of matched candles and pots of blooming bromeliads.

Use the warm colors of the flowers outside on a fall day to select the paint colors to brighten a room.

Branches with faux berries can be used as accents in bathrooms where there is no natural light.

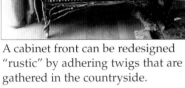

A cabinet front can be redesigned "rustic" by adhering twigs that are gathered in the countryside.

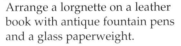

Arrange a lorgnette on a leather book with antique fountain pens and a glass paperweight.

Achieve the comfort of instant age by first bleaching, then tea-staining fabric for a warm mellow quality.

Style books by arranging in flat stacks and on end. Add small items for interest at every level.

Leave beautiful windows undressed, except for a pot of luxuriant creamy blossoms.

Dry herbs upside-down and flowers in a cool dry spot in the house for use in cooking and potpourri.

Stencil, stamp, or handwrite script as a decorating element to add character to the room.

Set the table for a holiday dinner by placing art pieces on the table until guests are ready to be served.

Small "personal touch" designs can be stenciled at random on walls or on lightly designed wallpaper.

On a dining-room shelf where dishes are stored and displayed, add an unexpected picture frame.

Paint an old limed oak table a soothing color and lightly distress for a new-fashioned heirloom.

Line pots of herbs in the window in the kitchen to make an easily accessible indoor garden "tasteful."

Old rose is a color of preference for cottage decorating to combine with paisleys, florals, and toile.

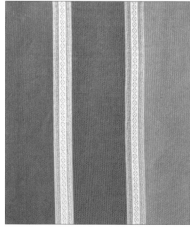

Antique fabrics found in flea markets color a vintage decorating theme, even if only as accents.

Stencil delicate garden designs on a wall in the kitchen area to soften cabinetry and appliances.

Hang vintage pictures high on the wall so that the top of the frame leans away from the wall.

Porcelain sinks, backsplashes, and accessories can be hand-painted by professionals to match ceramic tile.

Drape an inviting quilt over the back of a chair so that it is always available on cool fall evenings.

Tie tassels of the lamp shade color around a plain shade to add Victorian style detail to a lamp.

When selecting carpets, fabrics, and colors, gather all samples in the room to study for a day or two.

A single pillow placed against the back of a chair offers a comfortable welcome to a visitor.

Set a fall tablescape using a varied collection of colorful, themed items indicative of the holiday.

If your home has a wide hall area, place a love seat to act as a window seat reading or visiting area.

Overdo your decorating for the holidays of fall to help give thanks for the bounty of the seasons.

On every family vacation, buy a single vintage plate, then use this collection for family gatherings.

Display vintage hats on old hat stands on a dresser top or on a shelf near a much-used closet.

An antique pewter candlestick, decorated with seeds, greens, and leaves is an eye-catching accent.

To make a wall dramatic, install a wooden mantel between two windows and decorate as a focal point.

Create unusual wall patterns for "wallpaper" using leaf motifs and several different colors of paint.

For style interest, select each chair at the kitchen table to be different in style or color from the others.

Use an old glass lamp shade on a new base. The shade can be painted with glass paint to fit a decor.

Hang a framed vintage mirror next to the sink and immediately above the towel bar for stylish reflection.

Distress a wall area in a defined area for a shabby-chic-style backdrop to a sun room or porch.

Bring the garden right up to the back door with engaging sculpture and vibrant plants for transition.

Hang a small bell outside of your front or back door to welcome visitors or to bid a cheery farewell.

Use the delicate colors of nature to inspire your palette for fabrics and wall finishes. Brits love their roses.

"Hide" a small stone seat somewhere in the garden so that it can be "discovered" by garden visitors.

Plant massive areas of the same flower in borders around your home for continuity in lush style.

Large containers can be placed on each side of stone steps and the flowers changed with each season.

Pictures of famous paintings from posters and coffee-table books can be framed as wall art in cottages.

Place a small table between two windows and decorate with fresh flowers beneath a framed picture.

"Stain" raw wood with a mixture of latex paint and water. Desired shade will dictate water amount.

Victorian Cottage Style

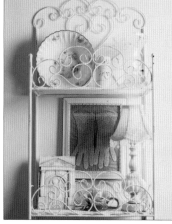

Victorian decorating allows you to go a bit "over the top" in styling with textures, flowers, shells, "dripping with crystal" lamps or chandeliers, lace, and frilly detail. The delights will come in styling "surprise" and personality into your home and garden.

Suspend a lightly scented handmade ribbon heart from a brooch on a shelf front. Add a bouquet to a table that can make every meal seem like a holiday. Frame a pair of your grandmother's evening gloves and hang them behind a collection of her things. Use a hand-embroidered tablecloth as a café curtain in any room where you wish to block or disguise the view. Wash an old dresser with white, distress it, and display collectibles.

Tie a delicate silk flower to the handle of your guest-room door to show guests which room is theirs. Cover an armchair with an old chenille bedspread and accent with vintage lace doilies on the arms or crochet-covered pillow accents.

Display miniature collectibles such as this embellished Victorian cup, small chest, and sewing plaque.

Wide tonal stripes can easily add a hint of a lighter more-modern look to balance a very Victorian theme.

The colors of rich silk flowers can be duplicated in bedding, window coverings, and tints of paint.

Frame a contemporary much-loved piece of jewelry in an antique frame and lean it on a shelf.

Use old books to act as a pedestal to display delicate handmade items on a shelf in any room.

Use exquisite bottles at eye level to make a beautiful grouping with an emphasis on shape and detail.

Accent everyday items with vintage fabric scraps and luxurious embellishments in groupings.

Stack a wire basket of berries atop another differently styled basket to suggest a picnic atmosphere.

Fill a white wire basket with red glass Christmas ornaments and a spicy candle to display all year.

Hang an old ladder in front of window and from the rungs hang antique linens and vintage hats.

Use a pale palette as a background for elaborately stylized designs to unclutter the overall room design.

Add a bit of romance to any country room, using a warm toile-fabric print on an accent wall.

If finials are missing on salvaged chairs use miniature enamel vases and accent with a beaded tassel.

A delicate beaded box lid begs to be touched. Accent with ribbon roses and exquisite mini frames.

Frame unusual pieces of lace with other bits of ribbons and beads to create collectible pieces of art.

Frame vintage wallpaper, and hang from a larger empty frame, then lean on a wall shelf.

Soft tones and muted colors promote a quiet, sophisticated cottage atmosphere of aged elegance.

Copper colanders and tureens make practical and beautiful countertop storage for garlic and onions.

Salvaged antique tiles can be used as trivets or as display backdrops with vintage china tea sets.

To make ordinary shelves memorable, discreetly staple bands of wide ribbon to the shelf front.

For style surprise, mix contemporary glass dishes with vintage ware that is complementary in color.

Stack cake pedestals, graduated by size, and weave seasonal ribbons to display on a dining-room hutch.

Glass shelves to display collectibles can be easily added to windows to obscure a view and add privacy.

Elaborate formal wallpaper can give a plain cottage room a charming touch that is not overstated.

Antique wash basins can be used as originally intended or double as a salad bowl and water pitcher.

Discarded trays can be salvaged and hung in groupings on a wall in place of other framed art pieces.

Layer an ironstone place setting and top with a damask napkin secured in a beaded napkin ring.

Cards of old trim can be used as once intended or displayed unused in a sewing or work room.

Remnants of old draperies can be used to make pillows, table runners, or single curtain panels.

Graduated hall tables can be placed in front of windows to bring flowers and color indoors.

Center an antique game board on a mantel between paired art. Flowers hide an empty fireplace front.

New dishes that replicate antique designs are oftentimes much less expensive to collect and enjoy.

Use a wooden china rack on counter or sideboard to display a set of mismatched vintage plates.

Keep the dining-room table simply decorated so the floor covering is the bold and colorful focal point.

Hide an ordinary dishwasher front with a café curtain and valance made with vintage textiles.

Old lace tablecloths can be thrown over the back of an overstuffed chair to add a touch of nostalgia.

Antique colored bottles lend an elegant touch to a serving tray offering wines and liquors.

Floral wallpaper is a background that is appropriate with almost any cottage or Victorian theme.

Create a "retreat" on a back deck or patio that can be used for quiet afternoons or intimate evenings.

Make a grouping "work" by keeping to color and theme. Here yellow and flowers combine.

Line plain wooden shelves with remnants of discarded lace or edging to highlight heirloom dishes.

Hang a dress on the "outside" of the closet door and embellish it to act as a part of the room's decor.

Small wreaths can be made from vintage buttons or jewelry and used as a sewing-room accent.

Use pieces of tapestry fabrics as dresser scarves, shelf liners, pillows, or arm-chair covers.

"Dress" stacked-towel shelves with lace edged guest towels, vintage talcum tins, tiny collectibles.

Use the color of the favored flower in your garden as a palette to paint garden furniture or cover cushions.

Paint and stencil an old table and matching chairs to echo the colors of the fruits in the garden.

A foliage wreath is in style in a Victorian decor outside or inside. Accent with real or silk flowers.

Embellish an old door or shutter with filigree metalwork for an ornate outdoor style statement.

Salvaged garden art is a tradition worth keeping on display for new Victorian-style gardens and patios.

Patio buffets for a casual brunch go Victorian with the addition of lace, porcelain, candles, and topiaries.

Secure wrought-iron elements, sconce parts, or chandeliers in layers for Victorian-style wall "art."

Elements from old Victorian gardens can be duplicated with small reflecting ponds and statuary.

Stake metal candle "flowers" in garden beds to bring romantic ambience to evening patio parties.

Echo the graceful shape of the vase in the crystal goblets and match the drink to the hue of the flowers.

Collections of porcelain in sweet groupings are shelf artistry for dining rooms and entry halls.

Arrange elaborate jewelry, delicate floral fabrics, and unusual touches for dressing table vignettes.

Lean an empty frame against a bathroom wall and accent with a delicate ribbon wreath.

Floral fabrics in rich Victorian patterns and colors can bridge styles with traditional design stability.

For Victorian bedrooms and the lady's dressing area, pastel florals and roses are feminine magic.

If fresh roses have gone by, sprinkle dried petals, especially lovely at holidays with Father Christmas.

Make an ordinary corner a fabulous comfort zone with a charming chair, memo board, fringed throws.

For a very special occasion, place a small gift box on the plate of the person who is being celebrated.

Frame a monogram with bits of lace, buttons, and ribbon roses and set on a shelf surrounded by fabric.

Antique radios paired with Victorian porcelain and vintage art make ideal style statements.

Victorian lighting was dramatic. Consider dimmers for special spots in your home to give more style.

Showcase antique albums and fine needlework set up as a miniature museum on an eye-level shelf.

Victoriana extraordinaire are these fancy metal stoppers and shell teapot, quite displayable as art.

Metal Christmas tree displays can be used for holidays throughout the year to display treasured items.

Arrange a dressmaker's dummy with lacy dress and a summer hat at the open door of an armoir.

Use a vintage piece of embroidered material, accented with odd pieces of lace, as a window shade.

Delight a child with a bed table set for tea, a baby dress, and a hand-made doll to dress up a bedroom.

Formal symmetry and opulent appointments such as rich woods are basic to Victorian high style.

Murals in a frieze effect were common in Victorian times and are coming back in retro rooms today.

Coffered ceilings, elaborate chandeliers and symmetrical window treatments are very Victorian.

Use rich color, figured wall coverings, Victorian furniture and beaded lamps to recall an elegant time.

Cross-frame ceiling beams, heavy textures, and high-style furnishings can recreate the Victorian period.

Carved newel posts and embellished staircases with sconces to light the way can be replicated.

Style tapestry fabrics draped, puddled on figured carpets, and elaborately tasseled for focal points.

Create conversation groupings around decorated fireplace mantels and use beaded shades on lamps.

Dining areas should have Persian carpets, lace tablecloths, and sumptuously upholstered chairs.

Nothing is more Victorian than a lady's "toilet" of matched porcelain pitcher, wash basin, and service.

An antique footed ewer in blown or molded glass is a classic Victorian element to display.

Carry the eye upward with shelf-display vignettes of stacked hat boxes, pedestals, and pots of roses.

Bring out the silver tea service and display it on lovely cutwork linen table scarves and centerpieces.

Beads and candles recall this high-style period. Turn a tiny shade upside down on a candlestick.

Frame heritage family photos in period frames on a tribute wall of a study, foyer, or lengthy hallway.

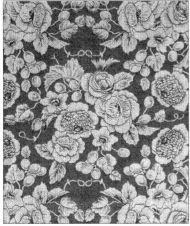

Figured wallpapers and fabrics in blue-and-white flower patterns are typical of Victorian cottage style.

Embellish guest towels and pillows with lace trims and crochet or embroidery work, white on white.

Use glass domes for displaying delicate treasures and group with fancy little framed photos and art.

Enhance a retro kitchen with windowed cabinets, antique hardware, and pristine white cupboards.

Finish cabinet tops with cornice trimmings so typical of the Victorian style practical beauty.

Enamelware pans and pitchers and Art Deco salt and pepper shakers add detail to retro kitchens.

Promote the porch pleasures of a bygone day with wooden rocker, and balustrade-style railings.

Transparent flower effects in wallpapers and fabrics are a lighter treatment for bedrooms and baths.

A rocker in a bathroom with a claw-footed cast-iron tub and flower stands complement period details.

A white picket fence and a bower of climbing roses finishes the garden for a Victorian cottage.

These traditional balusters, when put in a curved balustrade and painted white, are very Victorian.

Create a delicate wire hanger with curlicues and beads to suspend a scented votive candleholder.

Combine retro tilework with porcelain pedestal fixtures. Add a striking stencil border.

Use fluted-glass chandeliers, four-poster beds, frilly-edged window shades, with pretty quilts.

Layered area rugs to enhance hard-wood floors and carved-wood lintels.

Swagged windows, dark-wood mantelpieces, and friezework wallpapers complement cottage style.

Drape a corner table in textured velvet. Pair it with a velvet-upholstered chair adorned with tassels.

Embellished pillows plumped in leather and upholstered wing chairs spell Victorian comfort.

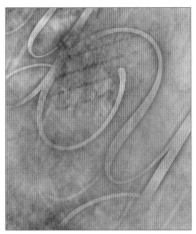

Calligraphy employed as an art form for wallcoverings is a way to personalize a cottage bedroom.

Emphasize stained glass, hard-wood floors, and corniced architectural details with minimal styling.

Round and oval frames, tiny wall-mounted shelves, and stenciled wallpapers are distinctly Victorian.

Add a pedestaled-sculpture group to an architectural feature at an entry or a garden transition point.

Overgrown fence rows with iron-work and cobbled paths are the ideal Victorian cottage ambience.

A hidden gate, out building, or entry to a home from the garden is mysterious approached in foliage.

Stone containers, mini ponds, basins and fountains are perfect enhancements for cottage gardens.

Romantic statuary in the Victorian cottage garden is an absolute must for an authentic accessory.

Expose old foundation stones and rock walls on period-home proper-ties for a time-worn appearance.

Flagstone or tile entries are ideal areas to receive topiary shrubs in groups of terra-cotta pots.

Stone stairs with rock "mosaics" for risers have a timeless appeal invit-ing a climb along a garden border.

Waxy leaves and red berries are perennial ornamental statements in a Victorian cottage garden.

A bronze or cast-iron door knocker on a hardwood door has an appealing cottage welcome.

Shells, stone carvings with elaborate detail, and cornices above entries can be replicated today.

Draw attention to a lovely garden sculpture by placing it in the center of a patio with encircling bricks.

A small tin can with elegant miniature porcelain roses is a nice Victorian contradiction.

When planting hydrangeas, mix two or three colors together and space so it appears to be one bush.

A garden bench need not be sat upon to be a focal-point style statement in the garden.

Moss and ivy-covered stone stairs, rock walls, and patios should be encouraged in the cottage garden.

Wherever possible, use rocky outcroppings and lush foliage to echo the British countryside cottage.

Brush the risers of stone steps with buttermilk and seed with moss or groundcovers to delight the eye.

Blue & White_ *Style*

Cool blue comes in many nuances from crisp and brilliant to subtle and calming. Paired with white the combination is always as fresh as a morning breeze. It is a color scheme basic to cottage styles, seaside decors, and even "big sky" mountain retreats.

Blue performs well in large areas, such as painted walls, ceilings, and tiles, or as an accent—perhaps a Delft clock or one's front door. Keep in mind that there are as many variations of whites as there are manufacturers of tiles, flooring, fabrics, wallpapers, and paint chips. For your vision clarify if your white needs to be warm or cool. Cool will work best with blues.

In an all-white room, particularly a bath or kitchen, a bright blue face cloth or towel becomes a focal point. White porcelain is always at home in a blue-and-white color scheme. A simple white pitcher or vase emphasizes a blush of blue hydrangeas.

Make a small candle ring with strips of velvet, satins, and hand-dyed ribbons. Emboss candle sides.

Display Victorian period prints in antique frames for any room in the home.

In a blue-and-white kitchen serve morning coffee or tea on blue vintage dishware.

Create a montage of comforting homey items to grace the top of a well-loved armoire.

Walls can be washed with a transparent darker blue paint and stenciled with lighter blue letters.

Place a small rounded white vase "overfilled" with blue hydrangeas by itself in a window.

Who says brick walls have to be brick red? Whitewash them like beachfront buildings on the coast.

Blue-and-white decorating can be accented by natural colors and subjects found in the garden.

A textured wall of blue tints and shades is especially personal with a handwritten script design.

Sponge-paint one wall with three shades of blue starting with the darkest color, then stencil letters.

Diamond-patterned floor tiles in shades of blue can be a dramatic base to decorating in cool tones.

Casual bouquets look beautiful when arranged in blue-and-white porcelains and grouped.

A clear palette of simple blue and white marries well with a proper English style.

When painting trim white, choose a paint with a blue undertone. This will give a calm, relaxing feel.

Get double-duty from blue and white vases by turning them into cake plate pedestals.

Add a pair of vintage shutters and paint them blue to bring another touch of color to the outside.

Script lettering from gift wrap or a computer can be enlarged and decoupaged, then sponge-painted.

When trying to decide which shades of blue and white work best together, try these.

A game room or library in blue and white creates a calming effect that allows for deep concentration.

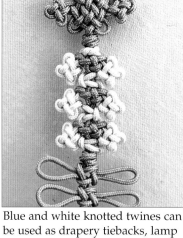

Blue and white knotted twines can be used as drapery tiebacks, lamp pulls, or pillow accents.

Decorate a front porch in blue and white so that even on rainy days it seems to be a summer afternoon.

Nothing is "cleaner" than the color blue, so place all of your cosmetic necessities in brilliant blue jars.

Begin collecting pieces of blue-and-white vintage dishes and display them on a white shelf.

A scarecrow dressed in "blue" jeans and white coat scares birds away and adds color to the garden.

White snowflake imagery stamped on a blue wall is extra "chilly" for holiday theme decorating.

A blue-and-white checked table-cloth is the perfect accompaniment for a homemade blueberry pie.

Blue is the color of "water," which refreshes and invigorates so use it in all accents in the bath area.

Use the tones of blue in nature to decorate the shelves in a sewing room or study.

A tiny touch of blue in an all-white room that is especially for children creates a soft calming effect.

Any wall surface, whether rustic or refined, can be enhanced by hanging blue "anything" on it.

Use shades of blue to paint baby blocks for a new baby that may be either a boy or a girl.

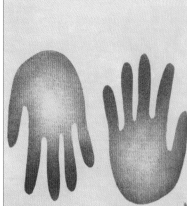

Dark blue handprints on an aqua background can be used on wall covering or bed linens.

Blue-and-white tassels are easy to make by using thin silk ribbon to cover two wooden beads.

Accent your blue-and-white collection of china with red-and-white table linens for a "new" look.

Give each member of the family their own shade of blue toothbrush to save confusion.

Showering in a blue-tiled or enamel-board area is refreshing. If tile isn't in your budget, roller-paint.

Avant-garde.
Style

Avant-garde style shifts our perceptions of color, form, function, and even geometry. Architecture defies gravity. This decorating style gives you a broad palette on which to stretch your creativity for the unique and unusual.

Color is dramatic, perhaps outrageous. From simple contrasts like black and white to hot complements such as blue and orange, color may be lively. It may also play stark areas or elements against natural and industrial materials. Architectural structures often set the scene for overall design and function. Struts, pipes, and beams may be exposed, often as they are or perhaps enhanced with black or brilliant color contrasts.

Simple shapes, textures, and lines within space take on new meaning. Tradition goes out the window in favor of creating rhythm, ease of basic functions, and always the element of surprise. Avant-garde is all about "minimal"—Less is more.

Faux finishes such as this one that resembles concrete are ideal for large areas or transitions to others.

Contemporary statues can stand or sit alone as the only decoration in a sleek uncluttered bath suite.

Paint a base of blue on the wall, decoupage cut out images of flowers, then lightly sponge-paint.

Style with hot color and unusual scale in soap or candy. A glass and wire trivet is unique.

In the kitchen use two ceramic coasters as a candleholder and a marble as a bottle stopper.

Hand-paint olives in tile squares on the backsplash in the kitchen in shades of green. Handwrite words.

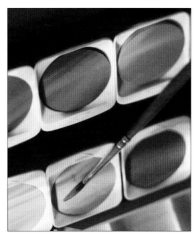

Avant-garde design typically uses colors from nature or straight from the paint box in brilliance.

Industrial-style lighting fixtures are perfect for the home interior decor of avant-garde minimalism.

Influenced heavily by the Japanese, textures of nature's foliage work well for wall or floor design.

Hang a gel candle in a glass bowl and suspend bright stained-glass and bead accents from its rim.

Separate rooms with textured bright red doors that have industrial or outdoor styled handles.

To make an indoor chimney give a dramatic room impact, faux-texture it to resemble wood grain.

Select two or three dramatic colors and design an entire living area, using only those against neutrals.

Combine horizontal stripes of wallpapers related in pattern and color value to "widen" a narrow wall.

For an attic room, cover the ceiling in reflective corrugated tin and paint the beams a bold color.

Do not add any accent pieces to a sleek living room where metal piping is the only accent needed.

A bar with no fancy bottles or glasses displayed and low contemporary chairs is nontraditional.

Paint the wall over a severe granite mantel dark purple and highlight with recessed spotlights.

Combining script, textures, and photo collages is a great way to personalize a wall space.

Let the architecture of a bathroom remain as unadorned as possible to emphasize a few dramatic features.

Textures of various-sized letters in layers of sponge-painted tones can replace traditional wallpapers.

Align three identical—except for color—lamps in front of "leaning" framed art and a candle for accent.

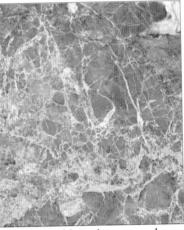

Marble, marbleized paper, and faux-marble effects make strong style wall and floor statements.

On a stainless steel shelf above the stovetop, line tiny glass vases all of the same color filled with flowers.

Various-sized numbers are as delightful to use for imagery as are letters for game-room walls.

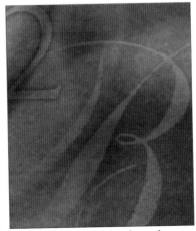

Rather than a jumble of numbers and textures, space them out by stenciling or stamping at random.

Create wire hangers, add beads, and then hang vintage lamp shades to act as candleholders.

Place two contemporary floor lamps behind the exposed back of a couch as practical accents.

Contemporary styling emphasizes large simple elements with glass and mirrors to add drama.

Decoupage overlapped, pressed foliage on a wall. Paint over all for a base, then layer up, and glaze.

Combining two or more ethnic styles can oftentimes be considered a contemporary approach.

Frame vintage silverware finds on a favorite restaurant menu or recipe in a shadow-box effect.

Line different colored earthenware jars on top of a cutting table for attractive storage.

In a large laundry room, build storage units that are partially enclosed and partially exposed.

Stencil alphabets over multitextured walls, insets on furniture, or closet doors of teen bedrooms.

In minimalist decorating, less is often more than enough. One small picture on the wall is just right.

Terra-cotta tiles, strong beam treatments, and granite counters create a spa-like environment at home.

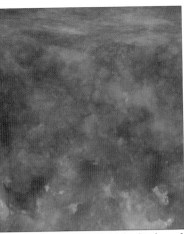

Sponge-paint a wall with shades of copper, bronze, silver, and a tiny touch of gold for metallic effects.

Serenity can be achieved with bare walls and highly polished floors. Use a few simple furniture pieces.

Textured effects can be created with sponge-painting or torn paper decoupaged in layers on walls.

Industrial lighting fixtures and structural elements support unique shapes and forms of furniture.

Simple is best for minimal impact styling. Smooth lines, little embellishment, simple furnishings.

A screen created from two doors hinged together is covered in squares of decoupaged wallpaper.

Secure four fir strips around an electrical insert on a balsa-wood base, glue parchment for a shade.

Uninterrupted expanses of hardwood for floors and ceilings may be kept rug- and drapery-free.

Spray-paint iron garden furniture a hot color for decorating punch and to act as a practical focal point.

Cola bottle art takes a new twist with combinations of stripes and angles for large graphic wall art.

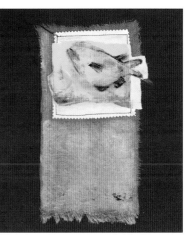

Handmade papers and fabric swatches can be layered and stitched for one-of-a-kind art.

Paint a black-and-white checkered border on a door molding between rooms, creating a framed effect.

The ancient Chinese established the power of red and black. Use it for avant-garde styling at home.

Steel-blue metallics are design textures from industrial inspiration. Use on floors, pillars, and walls.

Warehouse-style condos use distressed building features as style elements for entries and interiors.

A single giant numeral stenciled on a wall, door, or stair landing is a graphic element in metallic paint.

Why hide towels and tissue when a shelved caddy displays and makes accessible the practical?

Eclectic
Style

The eclectic style is always personal and works well for people of different tastes who share a space. Imaginatively combine unrelated items in fresh ways. Serve each person on plates of different design. Use small envelopes with button closures as gifts or frame as art. On a desktop, stack useful items—a bottle of lemonade and a lucky box! Top candleholders with flowered wire shades, add a glass filled with carnations. Hang old torn paper umbrellas from a ceiling to create a shabby-chic style.

Arrange kitchen shelves like store displays. Stack Fiestaware™ cups and saucers next to great packaged tea. Group a small vignette of black-and-white objects, books, and framed photos, then add a Fung Shui candle for harmony. Display framed children's drawings in a dining area. Place a small glass desk at the foot of a bed under a mirror to act as a makeup table or writing area. On a bookshelf place a glass bowl filled with water and a single fish, then accent with duplicate pots of small blossoms.

On a bathroom shelf place a ceramic art piece in place of shampoo and soap.

Hang an outside plant hanger on a kitchen wall and everyday cookbooks underneath.

In a kitchen, on a top shelf, line empty bottles in a row and top with fancy stoppers.

Stack paper-covered boxes on top of one another and use in workrooms where storage is minimal.

Edge dining-room shelves with broad strips of ribbon and line up stemware "bar style."

Old farm implements filled with unexpected accent pieces define the word eclectic.

Group a pair of goblets, a "dressed" bottle of spirits, and keepsakes on a guest-room tray.

Cut magazine pictures, frame between two pieces of Plexiglass®, then attach magnets for memo art.

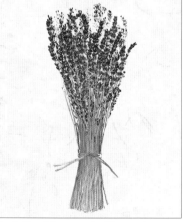

A stylized bouquet of lavender makes a lovely design for a backsplash border or individual tiles.

Use actual pressed leaves to act as stamps for wallpaper or fabric treatments in autumn colors.

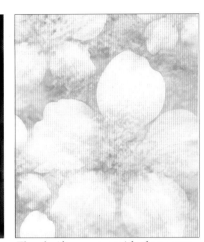

Paint votive holders with glass paint in floral designs rimmed with a lattice effect at their tops.

Floral gift wraps are ideal to cover hat boxes and waste cans to make storage and necessaries "pretty."

Paint closet doors with blackboard paint and supply young and older children with their own chalk.

Almost any style of wallpaper can be used as a backdrop in a room that is a collection of styles.

It started as a joke, but this fringed lamp shade on a mannequin-leg base is a favored home decor piece.

Eclectic styling employs a whimsical sense of humor. Hang boxing gloves in the family game room.

Create shelves in a bedroom or laundry room that resemble those in a fine department store.

Leaf shapes can be overlapped again and again in stenciled papers to lend design rhythm to a room.

Put a rocker with its back to a large open space to create a friendlier sitting room area.

If a lamp needs more height and visual mass, create a graduated book stack.

Paper doilies can be used to decoupage door fronts and shelves or tabletops.

Paint each chair a different bright color in an eclectic-style dining or family room where fun happens.

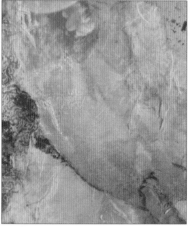

Walls can be painted with a water-color effect, using blending mediums or glazes.

Cover books with brightly covered taffeta, tie an oversized bow around them, then sit on bookshelf.

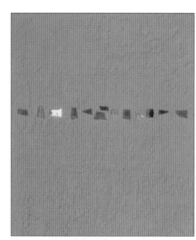

Create a wall border by plastering a wall; then while it's wet, adhere tiny pieces of cut glass in a row.

On a narrow wall area hang a long vase and fill with spring branches that extend into "other spaces."

In an eclectic room filled with treasures, pin cards directly to the wall, bulletin-board style.

Decoupage a wall with images that contain fruits and flowers, overlapping each exaggeratedly.

As a gift, make honey with rings of apples inside, cover with a circle of brown paper, and tie with raffia.

Empty colored boxes can be used to create a shelf effect on top of a table being used for a desk.

In a small child's room, create a bulletin board with tiny pinwheels with magnets on the back.

Old cigar boxes can be used for storage in a study, for jewelry in the bedroom, or kitchen recipes.

Stamps cut with pinking shears from old envelopes can be used to decoupage on the front of boxes.

A small collection of treasured items is nice to put in a corner of the kitchen countertop.

On a bathroom or guest-room shelf, place stemmed glasses that can be used whenever needed.

If you have a small inset window, treat it like a mini stage by adding draperies and figurines.

String a candlewick with hand-made beads to add that special touch for gift giving or decorating.

Subtle fabrics are necessary in cottage decorating to add stability to the sometimes overuse of florals.

Large rooms can be divided into "smaller rooms" just by the way the furniture is arranged.

Set up vintage vignettes of toys for decorating a child's room, displaying in a curio cabinet, or as accents.

Decoupage the outside of a square candle with wrapping paper, then trim with a gold metallic marker.

Stencil a wall by dividing the wall into sections, doing each differently to create an eclectic look.

Hang a large picture very high over the top of a large piece of furniture to increase the room's height.

In an eclectic decor Oriental style wallpaper can be used with Victorian, rustic, or modern accents.

Create a "crown canopy" for the master bed by draping yards of fabric from a wooden crown.

When serving meals, make them special by adding a collection of memorabilia to the table's center.

Design the top of a table by painting an array of items that are tied together only by color.

Frame a mirror in glazed metal and create a "bulletin board" with strips of ribbon lace and tiny clips.

Combine antique prints, doilies, and books with new touches such as these birds for a focal point.

Serve guests hors d'oeuvres and wine from a long hall table that is decorated like a photograph.

Hang small pictures in tiny nooks anywhere in the house to fill corners that may be too empty.

Paint cabinet fronts with bright colors, "unreal" sized fruit, and words to make each a work of art.

"Wash" a poster with a solid color and then add cutout words to the piece and frame or decoupage.

Select shades for a room, like these two darker colors, for floors and walls and lighter colors for accents.

Seaside Cottage _Style_

pale shrimp
Zinged with
limes & peppers

Olives in herbs
and Olive oil

Vivid Summer Veg

Gold Rose Soap

A seaside lifestyle can be the real thing or an echo of ocean breezes, gull music, and sand between your toes. As a decorating style, it's one of the easiest to emulate at home or in a getaway retreat. Whether or not you live near or travel to a beach, thrift and hobby shops have sea flotsam such as coral or fish net to cull through and purchase.

With shells gathered from the surf or purchased in a novelty shop, your "beach front" rooms can sparkle like a salt breeze. Display shells in baskets, glue them to frames and lamps, use them as drawer pulls, or decorative embellishments on Styrofoam™ Christmas trees.

Other sea-life imagery can come into play too: starfish, sea glass, driftwood, fishing buoys and glass floats, lighthouses, crabs, shore birds, model clipper ships, and so on. By combining them with your existing decor, your personal seaside style can be ocean fresh.

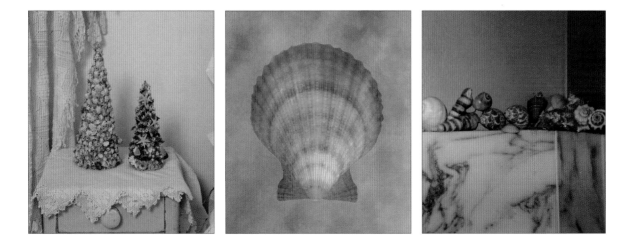

Small pictures can be made by gluing tiny shells to a paper with a design drawn in pencil first.

Cover an old mirror in the bathroom with shells that were collected during a walk on the beach.

Make napkin rings by gluing loose shells to mother-of-pearl, plastic, or metal rings.

Glue clam shells together around large Christmas lights and hang for romantic summer entertaining.

If your guest bath has a tile shelf by the tub, place a favorite piece of framed fabric on it to display.

Decorate the edge of a discarded birdcage with tiny shells and fill the cage with larger ones.

On a bookshelf, place candles made from candle gel filled with shells and a small turtle light.

Victorian shell wallpaper is a nice accent to a bath that has—or you wish it had—an ocean view.

Stack boxes and trays on a desktop. Adhere shells to the top of one box and fill tray with loose shells.

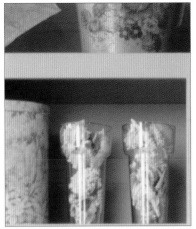

Fill large glass vases with assorted seashells and accent them with wallpaper-covered hat boxes.

For seaside decorating, select serving pieces and stemware that replicate the shape and colors of shells.

Recall a beach picnic with an old basket, a sunface trinket, sand, and arrange with a collection of shells.

Frame a special set of shells, then arrange with a pair of candles for symmetrical simple elegance.

Dinner plates for evening parties can echo the seaside theme by being in the shape of fish.

Create a vignette with a beach painting, boxes wrapped with raffia, shells, and candlesticks.

Place a table between two pictures and collectibles that are topped with treasures from the sea.

Pour melted wax and add a wick into the flat shells you have collected, then arrange them in a bowl.

Cover terra-cotta pots with shells and tiny starfish to use either inside or out on the porch.

A simple display of shells, branches, and wooden bird can be made from items collected on vacation.

Every seaside cottage should have a ceiling in one of the bedrooms painted to look like the sky.

Stack books on a chair to act as a pedestal for a favorite piece of art or a precious family photograph.

Make a garden border by placing clam shells in the dirt around the garden edge.

Two pots, stacked together and planted, can be filled with shells for accents.

For a seaside cottage, use collected rocks, crystals, and quartz in place of pinecones and woven baskets.

An aquarium can be filled with seashells if they have been thoroughly cleaned and disinfected.

Fill a vase with porcelain roses and marbles and the salt air will have no effect on the blooms.

Pale green walls with nautical words stenciled in one shade darker can be a subtle effect on walls.

Shades of soft blues and aquas can be combined in any room in a seaside cottage for a clean fresh feel.

Tile the walls as high as possible when living by the ocean to protect the painted walls from ocean air.

Unrelated images can be photographed or painted together and used as art for wall or furniture.

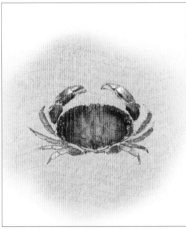

Create a small crab stencil and make a series of coasters for kitchen or dining-room use.

Wrap a tall candle with string, imbed small shells around the top rim, and hang shells from wick.

Leaves can be painted in varying colors of light blue, aqua, and gold and used as a stencil.

With this leaf stencil, the wall is washed in two colors and the stenciled leaves are painted white.

A faux finish that is as rich as this one is a nice accent design for cabinet fronts or furniture.

Stack all that is needed for luxurious comfort by the side of the tub for a restorative "spa" treat.

Create a contemporary picture of shells with your own camera, print them, age, and frame.

Hand-paint small sherbet glasses with glass paints and use for entertaining on summer evenings.

Delicate subtle colors such as these soften the harshness of the ocean sun and salt air.

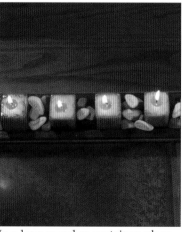

In a long wooden container, place square votive candles and polished rocks with engraved words.

Stencil two halves of a cupboard front, one right side up and one upside down.

Group houseplants in arrangements of three by varying heights, shapes, and container styles.

Add lots of pillows to a chair by a window so that guests can relax and enjoy the ocean view.

Decorate candles with wrapping paper, raffia bows, and beads and give to houseguests as a gift.

When choosing colors for decorating a seaside cottage, make certain they are soft and not too bright.

Use candy boxes from the "old days" at the beach in the bedroom so guests can "treat" themselves.

If you have a plain small cottage or guest house on the beach, paint with elaborate color and designs.

Small pictures may have little to do with the beach, but are perfect sea-travel accents.

Warm a room with the mellow colors of fall and suggestions of natural elements such as leaves.

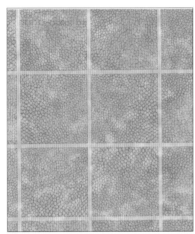

If you cannot afford to tile your walls, stencil tiles on the wall using an easy faux finish and thin tape.

Floral wallpaper and fabric are not typical of seaside decorating, but can be used for an eclectic feel.

Vintage games and toys can be collected and carefully used by adults who visit you at the beach.

At some seaside cottages the weather is often rainy; at these, paint walls and shutters bright colors.

Breakfast on the beach can be a party when simple miniature bundt cakes are served with fruit.

Tuscany
Style

For those who dream of Tuscany through travels or books or art studies, there is hardly an area more romantic on the planet. This central Italian area boasts antiquities going back to Roman times. Renaissance architecture and art at classical levels were established by Michelangelo, Da Vinci, Raphael, and others. Florence set the high-style of stone cutting in architecture with graceful arches, towers, columns, and breathtaking domes. Stone may be chiseled or polished marble, granite, or limestone.

Small religious shrines can be created in a home or garden by hanging a small box on the wall. Edge a meandering path with lush plants and statuary to soften hard lines and create a secluded passage. Enhance the view from inside with window boxes overflowing with colorful blooms on the outside. Garden statuary, incredible textiles with gold and silk fringes, and ornate tassels bring palatial splendor to homes of today. The finest in Italian style includes home and garden opulence from chairs to fences.

Hide less-desirable areas of the garden by planting a riotous mass of flowering shrubs and vines.

Hang found "art" or create a personal or inspirational plaque to welcome your garden visitors.

For contemporary Tuscan style, use elements of the Florentine countryside as art or to style a porch room.

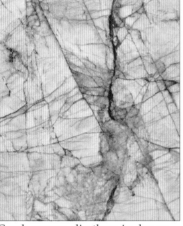

Crush papers, dip them in dye or paint, then use them to decoupage wall areas or cabinet doors.

Use broken roofing tiles to edge a garden path or to create a decorative mosaic on a garden wall.

Liven up a nondescript fence with a vivid coat of paint to draw attention to lush plantings in contrast.

Classical-themed statuary is a natural for any Tuscany style room or garden. Display even fragments.

Present guests with a wine display with hand-labeled Italian vintage years and vineyard names.

Outdoor flowerpots can be used indoors for cut bouquets by placing a hidden vase inside of the pot.

An actual or faux "aged" medallion can be added to a new home ceiling to give a dramatic emphasis.

Stencil a wall, overlapping stencils and using a glaze mixed with rich colors of yellow and brown.

Hand-stenciled designs can be added to beamed ceilings to make a room look rich and old.

Opulent wallpapers in rich colors can be used to add stately elegance to a formal room's design.

Repeat patterns in various mediums in the same space to give the overall design cohesiveness.

Paint a wall backdrop in rich Tuscan colors with an eclectic design and add Italian statuary.

Rich dark Tuscan woods are highly thought of and expensive. Emulate them in your decor.

Sponge-painted textures can be softened and aged by removing paint with a dry sponge as you go.

Decoupage calendar or poster art of Roman structures with rusty or bronzed glazes, then frame as art.

Tuscany *Style*

Antique iron or replica bathtubs can be enclosed cabinetry style in marble or faux-marble styling.

Secure a twig to a door or window frame and hang bead and stained-glass ornaments for sparkle.

Imply a sense of history with a Gothic arched door and wood that is aged and weathered.

Rocky outcroppings in terraced fashion can be encouraged to support moss and become focal areas.

Collect broken pieces of vintage garden art to add to a European style garden.

Renaissance libraries set the standard in Europe. Style with old books and book imagery papers.

Place a birdbath adjacent to a seating area on the patio to invite music into the garden.

A stone archway and a path leading through foliage to a secret destination harken to Tuscany.

Filigreed iron- and brasswork for a fence top or balcony railing is distinctively European in influence.

Border wallpaper can set a tone of lavish well being with ornate della Robbia fruits and mellow colors.

Decorate a dining table simply yet elegantly with two matching, very ornate candleholders.

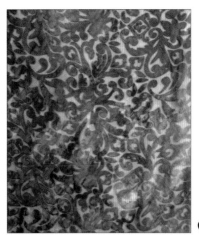

Sculpted velvet and rich tapestry fabrics are the epitome of Tuscan style for draperies and pillows.

Treat everyday items as art in small tableaus to create interest in forgotten alcoves—niche style.

Define small areas by repeating elements, like the round framed mirrors, in a variety of sizes.

Texturize the walls, using special paint techniques and naturalistic colors. Scrape areas for aging.

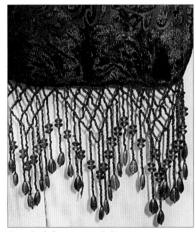

Beaded fringe in delicate patterns can enhance the most ordinary throw or drapery treatment.

Use warm colors and images of natural abundance to convey a sense of comfort and tranquility.

Place similar lamps or candles to the side of a framed piece of art to set the objects' color theme.

A wall sconce above an embossed tinware tray makes a stylish statement in a foyer or in a hallway.

Display shiny serving dishes on a simple shelf in front of a wall painted in mottled colors.

Alternately peg face cloths and hand towels at intervals beneath a mirror for abundant bath style.

A dramatic sconce-style lantern turns an ordinary entryway to the garage into a romantic adventure.

Marbleized papers and fabrics can be created in any color scheme to add Renaissance richness.

Hay-bale structural walls marry well with adobe architecture and a minimum of styling touches.

Rich velvets can be hand-stamped by using a vintage wooden fabric stamp and metallic paint.

Use an old church door as a front door and distress the sides of a concrete home to look aged.

To create a vintage look, evenly place a pair of small lights on either side of a paned window.

Roller-paint three or four colors on a wall and glue on pressed florals. Allow to dry and glaze over all.

To reflect della Robbia fruit porcelain, heap lemons in baskets or hand-painted bowls.

Enhance a carved wall frieze with old-world lighting. Fill a container with sand or pebbles, add candles.

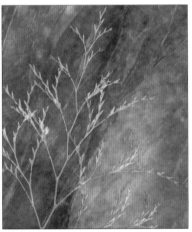

Pressed grasses and delicate foliage can be glued to wall areas and softened with sponged glazes.

The luscious colors of pastel sticks recall Renaissance paintings and tapestries. Study them for palette.

Beautiful glassware, leather lids, and brass embellishments, make container display an art.

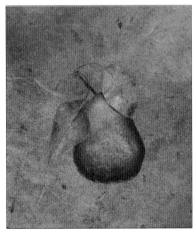

Ruby fruits are a della Robbia trademark. Use them everywhere in a Tuscany-style home decor.

Tassels with bead trim pair sumptuously with cut velvet and other tapestries in the Florentine look.

To lighten a Tuscany-style room, use a gentler approach to color tones and floral elements of design.

Shabby Chic Country_
Style

Quiet country living is the essence of shabby-chic country style. Understated embellishment, lovingly worn beauty, and washable surface treatments are typical of this style. Peeling paint, faded fabrics, and tattered lace recall an earlier elegance.

"Making do" was a phrase popular with our great grandparents during years of world war and deprivation. Sensible recycling and extending the life of furniture, with slipcovers and fabrics refashioned from sewing scraps, was a way of life. But style did not go out the window—far from it! Homemakers resourcefully created beautiful surroundings. You too can present the ordinary in an extraordinary manner for a shabby-chic approach to style.

Porcelain knobs and metal hand-rests on old panel doors are country "as is." Stay the urge to "fix up."

Use crocheted afghans and red-work pillow shams to say "country" on a wooden heirloom bed.

An unframed canvas with an oil sketch from a picture book makes a conversation starter on a mantel.

An antique gas stove is a terrific country element for the kitchen or porch, even if it no longer "cooks."

An old rake head makes for a unique utensil display rack in a retro country-style kitchen.

Use old wooden trunks and an ironing board in the kitchen to double for shelving units.

A plate-rack rod on a hanging shelf brings back country practicality on a charming scale for style.

Quilted squares are ideal place-mats for snacks on a country-white table setting.

Directly on a vintage tabletop, or on a foldaway hinged top, stencil a backgammon game board.

Cover a table with an old quilt, paint old chairs white, and display with a country icon such as a lamb.

Vintage quilts and pillows used to "countryfy" a love seat make an inviting reading area with a lamp.

A Victorian lamp sets a country high-style mood. Accent a chenille chair with a crazy-quilt pillow.

Quilts are always in style for country. Fold them, drape them, hang them, and complement them.

A pair of "shabby" chairs can hold stacks of country-style magazines on a landing. Hang a stylish quilt.

A jumble of bright pillows in various sizes are cozy. Make with fabric scraps and lettering transfers.

Quilts can be simple or elaborate in the colors you prefer, but they are an essential country-style element.

A simple quilted star in denim is an elegant statement of handcrafting skills returning to decors.

Near a comfy chair, arrange a magnifying glass with a few items that are just begging to be examined.

Serve tea on the front porch on a summertime Sunday morning with your best china and linens.

When planting, mix plants together so as visitors stroll through the garden there is an abundance of color.

Look carefully at the many shades in one flower and use those shades when choosing decor items.

Old logs can be recycled by cutting them into stool-height sections and matching legs to a table.

Bright clothes hung on a clothes line can be a wonderful "artistic" backdrop for a garden picnic.

Plant several blooming plants in one indoor pot and use on a patio or porch for continuous color.

Weathered whitewashed fence posts add a shabby-chic style to outdoor country decorating.

Small cobblestone-style pathways that lead nowhere are easily created in outdoor gardens.

The colors of the flowers in the garden can be repeated throughout the indoor country rooms.

Apple branches can be cut from the tree and displayed in sturdy vases inside the house.

An outdoor frog ornament is an unexpected way to serve fruit and snacks to family and friends.

Vintage button cards can be displayed by having them framed or simply pinning them to a wall.

Delicate flowers made from paper can be combined with twigs for an oversized dramatic arrangement.

Display items that are used often by a spouse in a place where they can be seen and enjoyed.

Attach small shells to the bottom of beaded lamp shades and display evenly beside a pitcher of flowers.

Vintage salt tins or salt boxes filled with sand or beans can serve as recipe book bookends or accents.

Hydrangeas should be included in your garden because of their color and beauty both indoors and out.

Vintage garden statuary can be placed in the center of a small pond on top of a cement pedestal.

Simple Country Style

The sweet life of the simple country style is farm fresh and comfortable. Art is hand-crafted and may be "folksy." Tinware, hooked rugs and pillows, crocheted items, and handmade quilts attest to this theme. Peg your mugs and cookware; fill a basket with red potatoes, purple and white onions, apples, or colorful squash. Antique coffee grinders and brass or enamel scales, often still in working condition, are practical as well as decorative. Children love to "help" with these anachronistic tools. Peg aprons on an old-fashioned clothesline to express simple country in authentic "great cook" style.

Simple country style can be sophisticated and elegant with chintz, checks, and plaids abounding. It can be down-home or rustic as well. Putting together a decorating scheme that rests on antiques or shabby-chic-style "rescued" items gives acres of room for personal style. In the country kitchen, what was needed in the way of tools and cooking ingredients wase generally at hand and in view.

A small Native American weaving can be used on top of a table to add color and ethnic influence.

Paper lamp shades can be painted or stenciled with country designs in the colors to match nearby fabrics.

A porcelain knob on a rustic-furniture door is more dramatic with a beaded pouch and tassels.

When clothing is almost too special to wear, hang it for a time on a line in front of a shuttered window.

Handmade dolls from different country regions and cultures display well in combination.

Worn jeans can be easily made into durable chair covers for the rooms of teenagers or younger children.

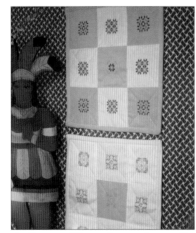

Antique quilts can be used as wall hangings or window coverings as long as the window is blacked out.

String gingerbread cookies or wooden cutouts in the kitchen or a dining area for the holidays.

An embroidered or beaded band can be handstitched around the side of a basket as an accent.

At the holidays, decorate each window on the house front with matching wreaths or candles.

Hang a large wreath on the outside of the house for fall garden parties. Stuff with live or silk accents.

Country garden trellis, arbor, or birdhouse elements painted white are always at home for this style.

A pot of blooming tulips can be displayed on an unused wicker piece to say "country" anytime.

Wicker and metal shelving can serve beautifully as potting stands on the porch or in the garden.

Old metal washtubs or laundry baskets can be stuffed with pots of herbs and annuals for focal points.

Place trimmed branches into a sturdy pot of soil, weave grape or other flexible twigs for a trellis.

The nostalgia of a weathered barn and an abandoned windmill recall long-ago country in framed prints.

Shabby-chic-style birdhouses can be tucked here and there about the garden for little surprises.

Two-tone candles are easy to make by simply following candle directions and using two colors of wax.

Crinkle brown wrapping paper, use as wallpaper, then sponge-paint for a perfect country wall.

A quilted piece that was originally made to be a table runner can also be used to cover a chair back.

Outdoor country artifacts can be used as functional pieces in untraditional ways indoors.

Match the colors of country fabrics to the colors of nature and use lavishly in country decorating.

Found antlers can be used above contemporary wooden blinds to add a country accent.

When plates are stacked on open shelves, use them as "display" areas for smaller handmade pieces.

An old picnic basket or overnight case can be display space for a teddy bear and someone's socks.

Dark deeper tones in stripes and plaids offer a bold solid background to country decorating.

Parts of old Mexican metal lights can be used with candle stands to create new lighting fixtures.

Stacked books can be turned page-side-out for a more interesting by contrast textured appearance.

Weathered boxes, tins, and rustic-style candles work well with old wood and hooked pillow tops.

Display old class and team photos with small antique items to create desktop interest for a study.

The beauty of Shaker styling comes from simple, practical furniture elements like these drawer knobs.

Fill an open chest at the end of a bed with an array of ruffled pillows and quilted runners.

Open a drawer to create depth interest. Use it for a surprise display space for candles or figures.

A variety of old books stacked at angles are a study in themselves. Use them as "pedestals" for objects.

A basement room can have a chalkboard painted on the wall and be used by children for fun or school.

Simple Country *Style*

Use vintage pickle jars to hold kitchen baking utensils that are used on a daily basis.

Old wagon wheels, tin buckets, horse harnesses, and screen doors make for country-style decorating.

Cupboard doors and open shelves can use whimsical plaques to keep children from easy access.

Tie bundles of herbs by their stems for drying and decoration, from a stick tied with raffia for pegging.

Tell a mini-story with a "forest" of bottles and trees and a tiny Swiss cuckoo clock hung on a bottle.

For a Christmas focal point, fill the cavities of antique toys with frosted gingerbread "passengers."

Hooked rugs can be used as wall art, to throw over a large coffee table, or at the end of the bed.

There's nothing quite so country as a brick fireplace and a glowing hearth to invite with comfort.

Warm fall colors can be used to hand-stamp pressed leaves for a wallpaper area over yellow.

A brilliant collection of handwoven pillows brings comfort and style to an ordinary sofa in a rustic room.

An old pine cupboard becomes a focal point with vintage china and a Navajo blanket at its side.

Marry contemporary comfort and glass style with lodge elements like wood paneling and rustic lamps.

A metal or twig head- and footboard are ideal in a log-walled bedroom emphasizing lodge styling.

Wooden toys, be they authentic antiques or replicas, remind us of simple farm lifestyles of the past.

Tiered pot racks, a sideboard with pull-out rods for drying linens, and old crockery are simple country.

Artifacts that are representative of certain country styles can be displayed in untraditional places.

A rustic lodge look is accomplished with open rough beams, wood paneling, and stone fireplaces.

Make numbers for the front door by "nailing" thin copper cutouts to wooden cutouts.

Make a simple arrangement of dried hydrangeas next to two "like" vases of different sizes.

Greet guests at the front door with a hand-lettered Welcome sign. Add springy hearts with coiled wire.

Old buckets can be decoupaged with images from magazines and used for almost anything.

Display or suspend pieces that were used daily in country living to decorate in unexpected places.

Decorate before a mirror with miniature handmade accessories on tabletops, mantels, or bureaus.

Lean pictures against the back of a shelf and hang rusted tin stars from shelf fronts for added accent.

Make small shelves with country cutouts, paint with crackle paint, and hang on outdoor brick walls.

Place a rocker or two on the front porch to welcome guests to stay for a while and visit, like old times.

Bentwood and rustic garden furniture can be draped with blankets and quilts for inviting color.

Use a taller-than-normal table to accent a seating area that would otherwise go unnoticed.

Make special meals memorable by serving them as if you were someplace else, doing something else.

Paint walls to bring to mind the colors and the textures of nature and the out-of-doors.

Favorite photographs can be computer enhanced, enlarged, and applied as a wallpaper mural.

Wallpaper can be aged by wiping with a thin layer of both diluted green and brown paints.

On a shelf or bedstead top, arrange toys, tiny pillows, covered boxes, or little birdhouses as vignettes.

For a country feel, don't "arrange" purchased flowers in a vase, casually place what looks natural.

For parties and family get-togethers, serve food that reminds the guests of everything country.

Dress an antique bed in vintage linens for a guest room.

A vintage sink or a retro one can be enhanced with painted tiles or mosaics to make a style statement.

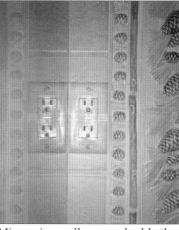

Mirrors in small spaces double the effect of relief designs on tile trims and backsplash borders.

Whether an old claw-footed tub actually is used for bathing, it's a style setter in a country bathroom.

Old-fashioned faucet styling is ideal with new ceramic or metal bar sinks set into old furniture.

Complement fancy tilework with hand-stenciled wastebasket and bathroom utilities.

A pair of boots or high-button shoes from long ago can take a turn as decorating footholds.

A log-walled room invites baskets or antique trunks to spill handwoven blankets for inviting texture.

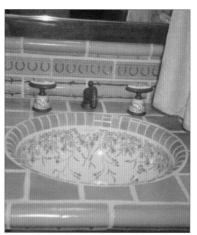

A charmingly painted basin and matching faucet handles take a bath from ordinary to fabulous.

A wreath of garden foliage comes indoors to style a mantel in a rustic room. Accent with lights or buds.

Shaker and mission-styled furniture pieces have a simplicity that fits with country and lodge rooms.

Where the stone of a mantel ledge is beautiful as it is, keep display styling to a minimum.

For a little decorative embellishment, knot a pair of tassels through round loops of door handles.

Drawers don't have to match within a time-worn chest. They may even get more style attention!

Use a masonry level indoors or out as a stylish spot for a vase of flowers and a mounded quilt.

Create a painted frieze of primitive animal and hunter figures perfect for rustic tiles on a mantelpiece.

Transfer a print image or decoupage a picture of a horse and rider to the door of an old chest.

Stone walls and mantels can be simply decorated with one or an odd-numbered few rustic items.

Soft lighting in a shelf area accents an antler used as a bookend and a grouping of family photos.

Simple Country Style

A simple shelf built on the upper third of the wall can display a collection of baskets.

Open shelving units in the kitchen are less expensive to install and act as a casual display area.

Loft rooms have levels of style and function that use ceilings as transition areas where walls usually do.

A hardwood slat or spindle bed and armoir are well suited to country style. Pile on the pillows!

When beautiful windows and walls are the focal point, keep furniture simple and comfortable.

Recall a sunny farmhouse with cozy seating, handmade rugs, and white-trimmed woodwork.

Drape or snugly pile throws in textured prints to bring comfort to any country seating environment.

Mission-style furniture, unique wainscoting woodwork, and muted lighting bring out country.

Beautiful simple wood cabinetry is in traditional contrast to children's tile art for a surprising bathroom.

Stack pillows of different fabrics, different styles, and different sizes to create an eclectic country look.

Log furniture's massive qualities set a room decor that can handle bold color and creative lighting.

A country bathroom with today's convenience can still have a few defining wilderness elements.

Stone fireplace walls and beautiful beams set the focal point for a lodge-style conversation area.

A strong log staircase can handle newel post treatments of Father Christmas or three kingly figures.

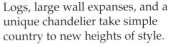

Logs, large wall expanses, and a unique chandelier take simple country to new heights of style.

An entire tree composes this awe-inspiring mantelpiece, perfect with rustic furniture and antlers.

High beams and wood supports draw eyes upward to stained-glass chandeliers and other home levels.

Intricate log-pattern styling can take advantage of many directions of architectural planes.

Additional candles are displayed by tying the two extras together with harmonizing ribbon.

It's okay to mix contemporary art in a simple style with the decor of a country "in spirit" room.

Homemade-appearing sand candles grouped in threes add a warm glow to wooden surroundings.

Wallpapers with cooking ingredients like grandmother once used are perfect for country kitchens.

A large wooden bowl holds different-sized and different-shaped yet matching-in-color candles.

Bright complementary colors and simple imagery set a "get down to the basics" lifestyle emphasis.

Stack a small stool on a chair in the corner of the kitchen and then add your favorite collectibles to accent.

Aged textures for walls, relief friezes near the ceilings, and warm colors are comfortably country.

A sponge-dyed terra-cotta vase is overflowing with moss and dried red roses for old-fashioned beauty.

Stencil red, white, and blue stripes and stars to embellish a weathered chest or table for outdoor style.

A distressed trestle-style table and ladder-back chairs are as tradition-al country in styling as it gets.

Tartan or otherwise, a fringed plaid shawl is a classy throw to drape over a sofa or a rocker.

A cabin in the country may be made of logs, but with mirrors and lighting it's up-to-date in comfort.

Denim was our grandparents' work uniform. Recall it for chair covers and table runners.

Harvest colors such as pumpkin orange enrich the family-room walls with cozy comfort.

Shop junk shops for antique skele-ton keys. Pegged in any room, they are a simply grand country touch.

The barn-symbol folk art of the Pennsylvania Dutch reminds us that bright color is very country.

An old pump can be a garden focal point. Insert an aquarium water pump, and it's an instant fountain.

Do not be afraid to "adjust" your lamp shades so that they are angled and not perfectly straight.

Set a wreath on a shelf by a small wooden box that is used to display a candlelit family photo.

Miniature chairs are very collectible and if you have any, make certain that you display them.

Stand a vintage rack on end and stack matching votive candles in shelf manner, then set aglow.

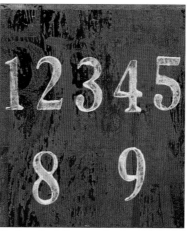

Red and white country hard to find? Roller-paint a red background and stencil white digits.

If your kitchen is vintage in nature add a twist by making a contemporary blender into a gel candle.

On a wooden wall, hang hand-dipped candles by their uncut wicks in the place of framed art.

A Fung Shui candle's glow and fragrance in a study can help to increase the power to concentrate.

Place tiny red wooden birds on top of curtain rods with curtains not quite open or closed.

On a tabletop, place an antique table runner to set off a candle with a metal heart tied to its wick.

On old wood, paint a coat of red. Let dry, then layer with green. While it's wet, scrape a design.

Primitive-style sketchy paintings of everyday items are whimsical for a country kitchen.

On an open kitchen shelf where glasses are kept, add French jelly glasses that are really candles.

Sit candles on the dining-room table, using pieces of china as a backdrop and a candleholder.

Decorate the lid of your teapot with a series of buttons and small metal roses. Display on a shelf.

To increase an aged appearance, stencil-paint layers on a surface, then scrape away in random style.

Use a sparkling glass salad bowl filled with marbles to act as a candleholder in a kitchen window.

Color with crayons, paint, then when dry, scratch images so colors showed through.

Hang a small fringed rug on the wall and use it as a backdrop for a shelf or tabletop display.

Wrap a chunky small round candle with corrugated paper and then tie with a ribbon "bow tie."

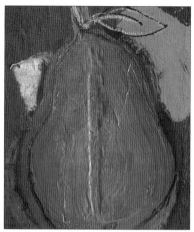

Painted and scraped layers of flat acrylics in red, gray, and yellow are "old country" effects to stencil on.

Beaded fruits strung on a cord embellish a "citrusy" candle. Pin into place near the wick.

Paint an old wooden box dark blue, then while it's wet, scrape in pear shapes, label on paper scraps.

Pewter and enamelware plates act as drip catchers and accents for candles you mold yourself.

In your own country-style guest room, light a candle and set out a sweet treat with a country novel.

For that Western "brand" look, stencil faux leather and glaze until satisfied with the rustic quality.

Choose a good read from stacks of fiction, a candle for ambiance, and stemware to hold a few sweets.

A comforter chest at the foot of the bed gets stitchery or stenciled lid art and offers put-on-shoes seating.

Hang metal stars over a doorway in a lopsided style. Place a few on the ceiling as well.

Arrange patterned enamelware and mason canning jars with a wooden recipe card box.

Photo *Credits*

We would like to thank the following photographers and photo resources for the 1001 images for this book.

Chapelle, Ltd.
Kevin Dilley, Hazen Imaging
Leslie Newman
Luciana Pampalone
Michael Skarsten
Jessie Walker
Scot Zimmerman

Artville LLC Stock Images (® 1997–1999)
Comstock, Inc. Images (© 1997)
Corbis Images (© 1999–2001)
Digital Stock Images (© 1997–1998)
Getty Images (© 1997–1999)
PhotoDisc, Inc. Images (© 1992–1996, 1998–2001)

Index

Index
Cont.

Letters can be primitively stampe[d] on a faux-finished wall and then distressed to appear very old.

128